A FIELD GUI

Little-Known & Seldom-Seen

Birds

of North America

A FIELD GUIDE TO

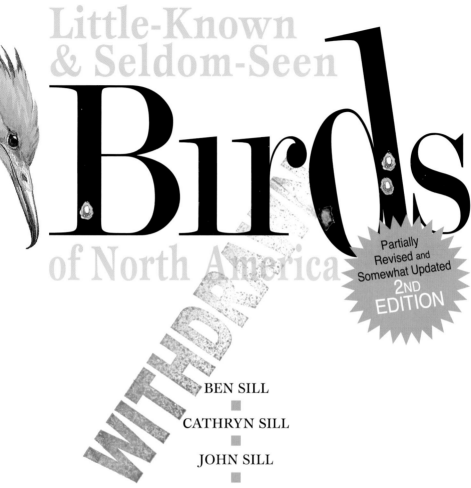

Little-Known & Seldom-Seen

Birds

of North America

Partially Revised and Somewhat Updated 2ND EDITION

WITHDRAWN

BEN SILL

CATHRYN SILL

JOHN SILL

Illustrated by JOHN SILL

PEACHTREE
ATLANTA

To the One who has given us
real birds that bring us
so much joy

Published by
PEACHTREE PUBLISHERS
1700 Chattahoochee Avenue
Atlanta, Georgia 30318-2112

www.peachtree-online.com

Book design and composition by Loraine M. Joyner

The illustrations were created in watercolor on 100% rag, archival watercolor
paper. Title designed with Microsoft Typesetting's Modern No. 20 and ITC
Esprit by Jovica Veljovic; text typeset in Microsoft Typesetting's Cambria by
Jelle Bosma, Steve Matteson, and Robin Nicholas; titles and headings typeset
in ITC Esprit; subheads and captions typeset in ITC Kabel by Rudolf Koch.

Printed in March 2013 by RR Donnelley & Sons in South China
10 9 8 7 6 5 4 3 2 1
Second Edition

Library of Congress Cataloging-in-Publication Data
Sill, Ben, 1945-
  A field guide to little-known and seldom-seen birds of North America / Ben
Sill, Cathryn Sill, John Sill ;
illustrations by John Sill. – 2nd edition.
    pages cm
  ISBN: 978-1-56145-728-1 / 1-56145-728-0
  1. Birds—Caricatures and cartoons. 2. American wit and humor, Pictorial. I.
Sill, Cathryn, 1953- II. Sill, John, ill. III. Title.
  PN6231.B46S54 2013
  598'.07234'0207—dc23
                    2013000874

CONTENTS

INTRODUCTION

W HEN THE FIRST EDITION of this Field Guide was published, there was much uncertainty in the birding community. Some of the new species described were a bit speculative, since little scientific data were available at that time. Now, twenty-five years later, we are pleased to say that the birds described in this updated volume are not only accurate, but also artfully arranged and sufficiently ambivalent. Simply put, this guide is the serious birder's best friend, but it will allow even novice birders to have an adjustable experience.

We are not too proud to admit that mistakes made in the first edition were the editor's fault.

The present guide clearly elucidates where newer studies have shown that original characteristics of certain species were incorrectly interpreted as being mistakenly accepted as unconfirmed fact.

LET IT BE KNOWN that we have been hard at work to stay ahead of the birding frontier. To make this obvious to users of the guide, we requested that the publisher let us rename it as A FIELD GUIDE TO LITTLE-BETTER-KNOWN AND LESS-OFTEN-SELDOM-SEEN BIRDS OF THE WESTERN HEMISPHERE, PARTICULARLY NORTH OF THE TROPIC OF CANCER, SOUTH OF THE ARCTIC CIRCLE, AND FOCUSED ON NORTH AMERICA, NORTH OF THE MEXICAN BORDER AND EXTENDING SOMEWHERE INTO CANADA. Much to our disappointment, this request was denied. Left with no other choice, we kept the original title.

The Field Guide

AN EXPLANATION

AS WITH ALL PUBLICATIONS of this type, the primary objective is to facilitate ready identification of a particular species in the field. This is usually accomplished by a combination of several factors:

1) a general description of the bird's appearance,
2) observation of its habitat, song, and range, and
3) actual identification by a well-respected birder
   in the group.

It is with some pride that we have scooped the many other field guides available today, none of which exclusively include new and seldom-seen species. Unlike these other "standard" guides, ours represents birding at its state-of-the-art best.

Some of the more important characteristics of this field guide are presented below:

1) As you expect in any quality field guide, this volume is replete with numerous accurate illustrations, detailed descriptions, observation hints, and range maps where appropriate.

2) We couldn't think of a second important characteristic, but you can't use numbered paragraphs unless you have more than one item.

A CONSCIOUS ATTEMPT has been made to eliminate the ambiguous language of other field guides. Our reader-friendly glossary includes a list of terms often found in other guides contrasted to our more lucid terminology. Remember that the most important thing in field identification is the name of the bird. With the name you can readily look up the bird in a field guide such as this.

BIRD NOMENCLATURE

WHILE EVERY ATTEMPT has been made to keep the text clear and simple, we understand that many birders will become confused with the technical nomenclature needed for the proper description of the birds in this volume. The illustration below shows a completely labeled bird.

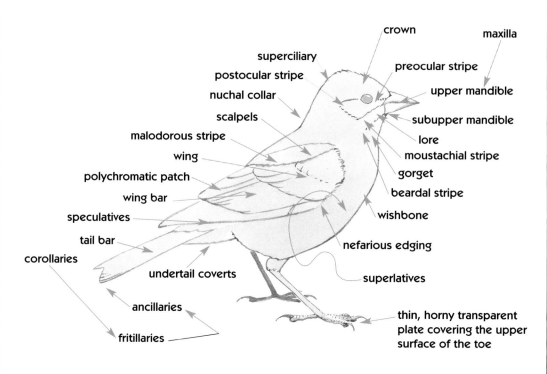

ACKNOWLEDGMENTS

S PECIAL THANKS are due to those individuals who used prepublication copies of this updated field guide for actual field verifications. However, when their data did not agree with our opinions, we deleted them.

Seriously, we would like to acknowledge the people at Peachtree Publishers who have worked so hard on the field guide. A special thank-you goes to Loraine Joyner for her creative ideas and to Vicky Holifield for her help in making sense out of our nonsense.

Warbling Cormorant

Little-Known
& Seldom-Seen

Birds

AQUA SECTION

Gila Gull

Apparently isolated when the prehistoric seas disappeared, this transient species is locally common in the southwestern United States. A secretive bird, it is typically observed only while feeding in flash-flood areas. While the Gila Gull closely resembles other gulls, it can be identified by its orange and black legs and the lizard in its mouth.

Song is a gargled *agua arriba! agua arriba!*

OBSERVATION HINT

The appearance of this bird is highly erratic and dependent on local weather conditions. Monitor an internet weather site and when thunderstorm warnings are issued, travel immediately to the nearest gulch or arroyo or gully or ravine or gorge and erect an observation blind. Be sure to note previous high-water marks.

Range

SPECIALIZED EQUIPMENT

Personal flotation device

Also illustrated: the Trans-Pecos Whiptail

Warbling Cormorant

An average-sized, dark bird, the Warbling Cormorant can be safely separated from its close relatives by its call and its inflatable throat pouch. This species, which is restricted to coastal regions, vocalizes only on foggy days. When vocalizing, the Warbling Cormorant expands its throat pouch to provide resonance, and draws up its wings to either side of its head to reflect the sound.

Its song is a low warbled *dru-ul-ully-ully-argh-hmm-ooah-ah-ahoo-dree-eee-ahwho-mmm-mmm* followed by several soft, rather random, lyrical phrases. Its call is a deep, booming *OOOH–WHAAA!*

OBSERVATION HINT

On foggy days, see above; on sunny days, wait for a foggy day and listen for the call. Once the warble is pinpointed, wait for the fog to clear for possible identification of the bird.

Warbling
Cormorant

Seed-eating Tern

This exciting bird is much more advanced biologically than its ordinary fish-eating relatives. As fish populations have been depleted, this opportunistic tern has acquired the ability to eat a wide variety of grains. *Plummetus granolium* is the only tern that has been able to qualify for "authentic vegan" certification. It is a spectacular sight to see a flock of these birds diving headlong into a wheat field from heights of up to 100 feet.

Call is a semi-addled *chaff chaff*.

AUTHOR'S NOTE

Within this tern's range, it is advised to purchase reinforced feeders.

Multi-toed Snorkel Bill
(formerly Four-toed Snorkel Bill)

An uncommon-to-rare inhabitant of intertidal marshes, this two-foot-long bird spends most of the daylight hours under water, going ashore only at night to dry its feathers. The Snorkel Bill may be tentatively identified by its vertically oriented bill, which moves rapidly with 2 to 3 inches extended above the water surface. It nests in shallow water on old fish beds with unusually high hatchling mortality rates. Due to projected sea-level rise, many shore-nesting birds may adopt this nesting behavior. Seldom calls. Range varies.

OBSERVATION HINT

Take up a location in a dense spartina (cord grass) tidal marsh on a calm day. Constant surveillance of the marsh fringes may reveal what appears to be a short, erratically moving reed. This is either a Multi-toed Snorkel Bill or a short, erratically moving reed.

AUTHORS' NOTE

These birds were so little known when the first edition of this guide was published that the authors thought it had four toes. We were wrong. We still don't know for sure—thus the name change.

Profile view

Ventral view

Middle Yellowlegs and Least Yellowlegs

Existence of these two new species was substantiated shortly before the first edition of this field guide went to press. Both are similar to the Lesser and Greater Yellowlegs; however, they are readily identified by the fact that the Middle Yellowlegs is smaller than the Greater Yellowlegs, while the Least Yellowlegs is smaller than the Greater, Middle, and Lesser Yellowlegs, but is larger than some smaller birds.

Very recent studies have shown that this group of birds may well contain even more species (not illustrated yet). The two most likely to be added to this genus are the Yellow Middle Legs and the Slightly Yellow Lesser Legs.

SPECIALIZED EQUIPMENT

To estimate sizes, it is helpful to insert yardsticks (meter sticks) in mudflats where Yellowlegs feed.

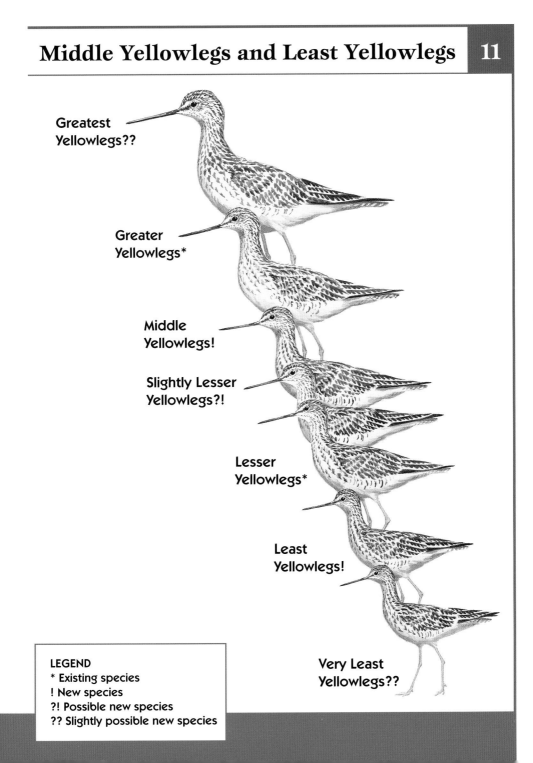

Greatest
Yellowlegs??

Greater
Yellowlegs*

Middle
Yellowlegs!

Slightly Lesser
Yellowlegs?!

Lesser
Yellowlegs*

Least
Yellowlegs!

Very Least
Yellowlegs??

LEGEND
* Existing species
! New species
?! Possible new species
?? Slightly possible new species

Auger-billed Clamsucker

At close range, the spiral grooves on the bill of this rare shore bird are sufficient to provide positive identification. Feeding is accomplished by inserting the bill into the mud until it encounters a clam and then walking in clockwise circles to drill the bill tip through the shell. The clam body is sucked out, and the bird rapidly walks counterclockwise to free itself. During feeding frenzies, an individual occasionally drills at such a rate that the entire head will disappear beneath the sand. When flying into a stiff headwind, these birds tend to spiral.

The Auger-billed Clamsucker's song, a hearty *chow-der, chow-der,* is seldom heard. In the presence of birders, they usually clam up.

OBSERVATION HINT

Flocks of Auger-billed Clamsuckers often follow herds of migrating clams. Best results have been obtained by erecting blinds in spring and fall along either the Atlantic or Pacific Clamway.

Flight

Drilling

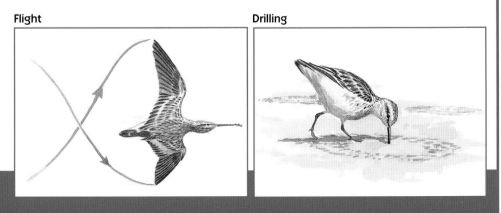

Long-range Target Duck

The Long-range Target Duck is one of the few examples of inverse evolution. The more distinct the markings on this bird, the more likely it is to meet an untimely death. The Atlantic population of this duck normally flew only 20 feet above the ground. Unfortunately this subspecies has been extirpated, leaving only the midwestern subspecies, which flies at 153 feet.

Its warning call is a frantic *duck, duck.*

OBSERVATION HINT

Once in your sights, this bird is easy to identify. However, it is difficult to gauge your chances of getting a good look at a Long-range Target Duck. At best it is a long shot. Use peep sights for the young.

ADDENDUM

Recently an additional subspecies has been discovered in southern Canada, where only a very few individuals remain. This bird has a distinctive red spot on its breast.

Omaha Dabbler

The only information about this species originally came from a single description supplied by a fisherman in Omaha, Nebraska. He sighted this bird on two different occasions: first, when it was perched in a tree, and next when it was feeding on a lake. Realizing that there was a gap in our data, we sent noted gap biologist John Garton to do some fieldwork on the Dabbler in 1988. After an extensive thirty-seven-hour study, his only conclusion was that the males of this species have a slightly larger dotted central portion than do the females.

NOTE FOR REVISED EDITION

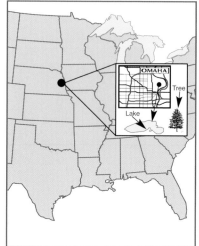

We were able to coax John Garton out of retirement with the offer of a mostly expenses-paid trip to Nebraska for five days and two nights to conduct additional research. His findings were a near revelation. Garton determined that the Omaha Dabbler has a bright red shoulder patch. This now leaves us with two smaller gaps. The scientific name of the Omaha Dabbler has been changed to Omahaensis bi-gapus.

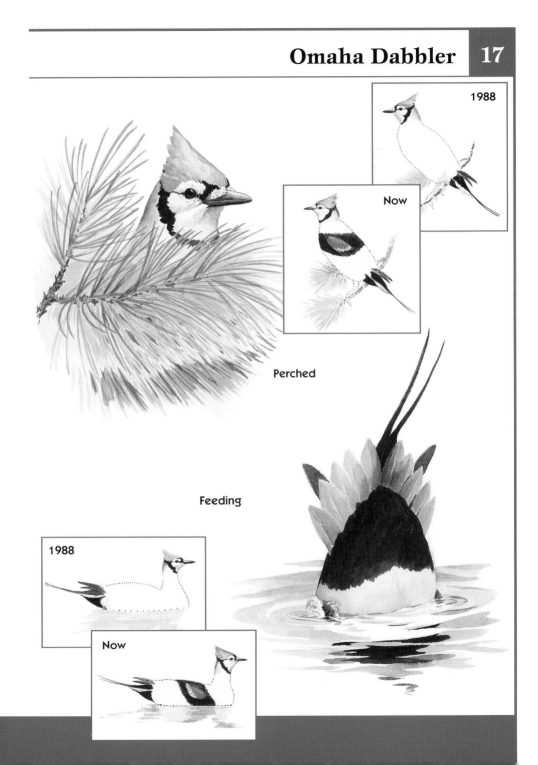

1988

Now

Perched

Feeding

1988

Now

Skia

This big-footed bird of shores, lakes, and mountains was once widespread in North America, but has now been fragmented into several subspecies. The north-eastern (Nordic) subspecies migrates cross-country, while the northwestern (Alpine) subspecies migrates downhill. The southern subspecies (Water Skia) is restricted to lakes and bays. Skias are interesting birds to observe in flight. Concentrations seem to occur in Calgary, Alberta; Vancouver, British Columbia; and Lake Placid, New York.

OBSERVATION HINT

Water Skias arrive after the spring thaw.

IDENTIFICATION AID

The various subspecies can be separated by their footprint, although the southern Water Skia is difficult to track.

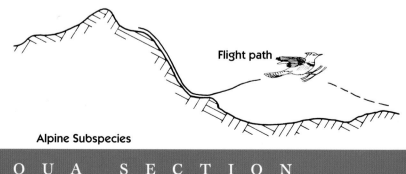

Flight path

Alpine Subspecies

Alpine

Nordic

Southern or Water Skia

Elegant Vulture

Southern Snake Strangler

This rare denizen of southern swamps feeds almost exclusively on water snakes. Classified as constrictors, Stranglers squeeze the daylights out of their prey, causing suffocation. (In years with low snake populations, birders have observed the bird trying to strangle turtles.) Often two or more birds combine efforts to kill long snakes. This cooperation, rare among birds, is called "team suffocation."

OBSERVATION HINT

This bird can be decoyed by placing a rubber snake in an open area of the swamp. When the Snake Strangler finds the fake snake, it will often squeeze for days before becoming frustrated and giving up. During this period, observation is easy.

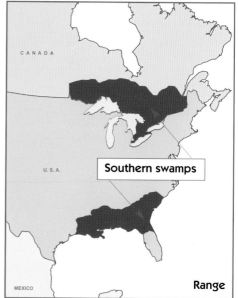

Southern swamps

Range

Team suffocation

Spring Kite

This rarely common, small bird of prey is easy to identify when hovering. The bird generally faces into the wind and can remain stationary even against a substantial breeze. Range generally excludes forested areas and electric transmission-line corridors, where mortality rates are high. Courtship displays include repeated looping, with an occasional sudden crash directly into the ground.

Perched

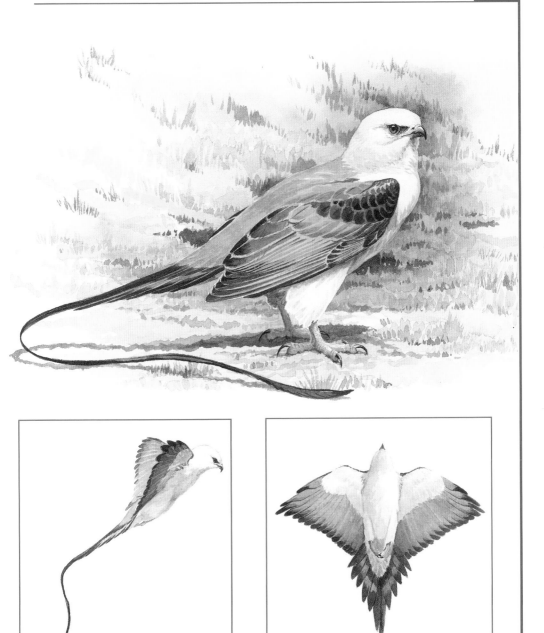

Adult

Juvenile

Elegant Vulture

Except during the extremely short breeding season, this bird has the appearance of a Turkey Vulture. The breeding plumage consists of a white neck ruff and a handsome flowing crest. Its soaring habits make it difficult to distinguish the Elegant Vulture from other vultures when viewed from below. To obtain views from above, close approaches can be made with hot air balloons; however, the birds usually leave by the time the balloon is fully inflated. The range of the Elegant Vulture coincides with that of less elegant North American vultures. Scientists have coined a term for this species' exceptionally short breeding period (May 3 and 4): "conjugal interruptus."

OBSERVATION HINT

The candy-apple red toenails of the Elegant Vulture allow it to be positively identified in all seasons.

View from above

Night-flying Teeter

Completely nocturnal, this bird has evolved to blend in with the night, which explains its overall dark color. It does this so well that the terms "darkness" and "teeter" may well become synonymous. Baby teeters, or teeny teeters, are crepuscular. Lacking their full quota of night camouflage, they are active only at dusk and dawn, when they cannot be seen. To date, this species, which represents an entirely new genus, is known only from a single road-killed specimen.

OBSERVATION HINT

This species is best observed when feeding on lightning bugs. Sometimes, however, these birds will begin feeding during a total solar eclipse, and may be caught afield after the moment of totality is past.

Optimal observation time

Type specimen

Ripped Grouse

Circular Dove

This medium-sized bird has evolved with one leg longer than the other. This leg-length disparity causes the Circular Dove to walk in circles, possibly providing an uncertain survival advantage. The western subspecies is identified by the fact that it walks in larger circles (670 km or 420 miles) than the eastern subspecies (314 miles or 502 km). Sexes are most readily determined by the fact that the males have a long left leg, whereas females have a long right leg. As a result, males walk clockwise, females counterclockwise, making breeding opportunities rather unpredictable.

OBSERVATION HINT

Because the flocks travel in circles, observations are cyclic. Stake out the location and wait. Based on a walking speed of 0.2 mph (0.32 km/h), the flock will return every 21 days (28 days for the western subspecies).

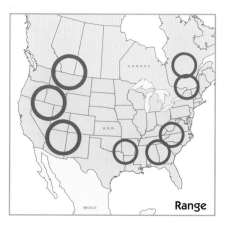

Range

♂

♀

At rest

Ripped Grouse
(formerly Waddley Grouse)

In a startlingly rapid change, the Waddley Grouse has transformed itself into a lean and fit gallinaceous bird. Environmental pressure exerted by hunters on the succulent Waddley Grouse has led to this transformation. The initial change began with a new diet of high-protein insects, fruits, nuts, and whole grains. A more active lifestyle of running and flying instead of sitting and eating also improved the bird's physique. The now sinewy bird is too tough for the table and hunting pressure has plummeted.

Grouse courtship is often showy but the Ripped Grouse has taken it to a new level. The males will pose, exposing the bare skin between feather tracts to show their remarkable muscle definition. Biologists call this behavior "flexing."

Waddley Grouse

Full flight

Full frontal

Blunt-billed Woodpecker

Great-toed Clapboard Pecker

This widely distributed member of the woodpecker family has the obnoxious habit of searching for food on the exterior of residential dwellings worldwide. One subsidiary subspecies, found only in suburban subdivisions, uses its great toe to grab gutters. In the southwestern U.S., this species has apparently hybridized with the Blunt-billed Woodpecker and is attacking adobe homes. Feeding activity peaks about an hour before the alarm clock rings.

OBSERVATION HINT

Build a house—anywhere.

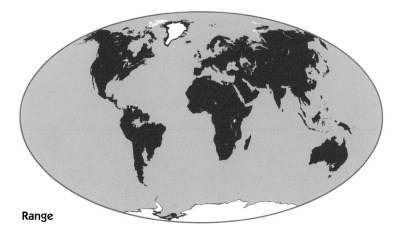

Range

Subsidiary subspecies

Ebony-billed Woodpecker

For years, ornithologists have misidentified this species, being led by a group of "splitters" who wanted to add numbers to life lists. It is only through a detailed study of this group that we now know that the Downy, Hairy, Acorn, Yellow-bellied Sapsucker, Three-toed, and White-headed Woodpeckers are actually only subspecies of the Ebony-billed Woodpecker. While the various forms exhibit some trivial differences such as size and plumage, careful analysis should have indicated that they are indeed a single species because all these birds have a common trait: a dark bill.

AUTHORS' NOTE

Many type specimens of the Ebony-billed Woodpecker have been found—scattered over most of the U.S. and much of Canada.

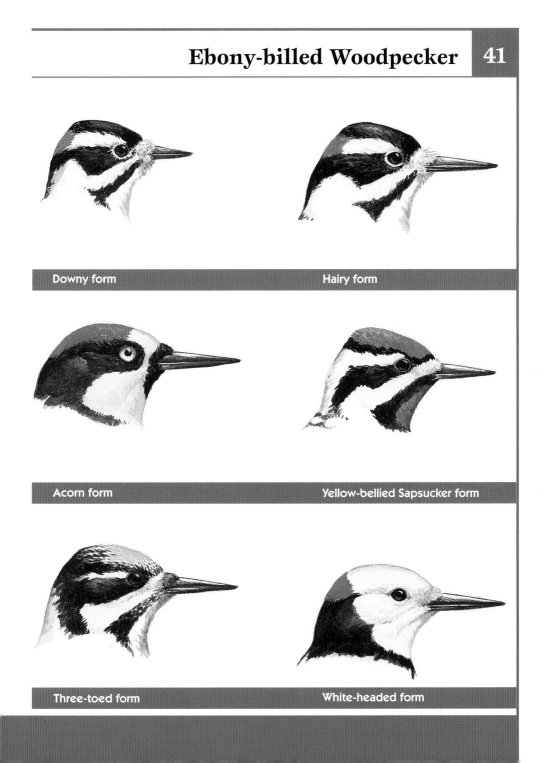

Downy form

Hairy form

Acorn form

Yellow-bellied Sapsucker form

Three-toed form

White-headed form

Blunt-billed Woodpecker

Rare and local, primarily due to lack of habitat renewal. The last remaining population of this medium-sized ladder-backed woodpecker is limited to a small area in the desert southwest. Fortunately, here it receives complete protection. Fallen trees usually serve as nesting sites. This bird feeds primarily on silica borers. While the bird is actively feeding, the eye color changes from its customary white to red. Flight is distinctive, often appearing as if the bird is spatially disoriented.

Song is a series of short moans.

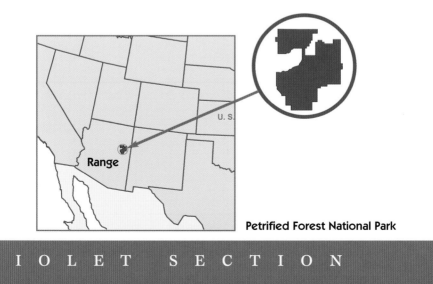

Petrified Forest National Park

Adult–8:00 a.m.

Adult–5:00 p.m.

Juvenile

Green Plumivore

White-lined Roadrunner
(formerly Macadam Roadrunner)

Believed to have evolved as a separate species only in recent years, this fairly large terrestrial bird is rapidly extending its range. Although widespread, its numbers remain low because of high mortality. It runs up to 35 mph (103,500 furlongs/fortnight), but this, unfortunately, is below the minimum allowable speed in its habitat. At present, populations are restricted to principal federal transportation corridors. Feet have a unique radial tread pattern.

Environmental noise can obscure the call, which is an occasional *beep-beep.*

SPECIALIZED EQUIPMENT

Road atlas

ADDENDUM

In the last two years, a new subspecies of this bird has been discovered on state and county roads. While similar in appearance to the White-lined Roadrunner, it has a solid yellow line down its back. For the present it is called the Non-passerine Roadrunner (Geococcyx alba-linearis bananaensis).

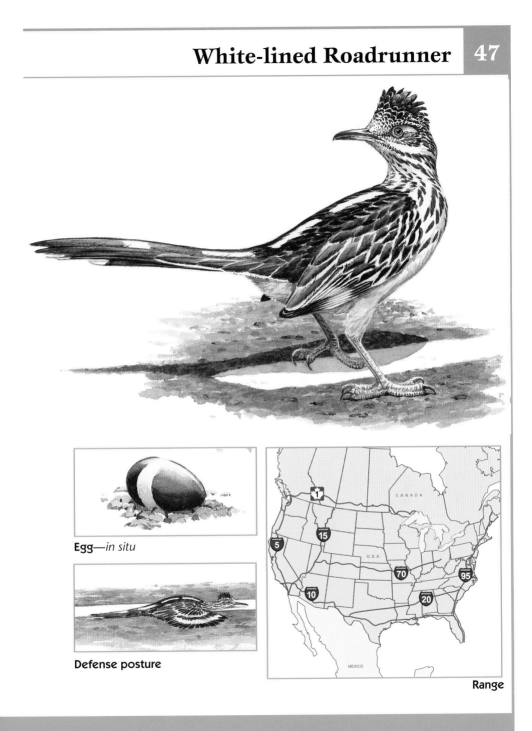

Egg—*in situ*

Defense posture

Range

Green Plumivore

A recent discovery restricted to reforested areas, it is the first avian species known to recycle. This bird actually eats the wing and tail feathers that it molts each year, a behavior known as "primary, secondary, and posterior ingestion." Without the need for external food sources, the Plumivore is essentially a perpetual organism; some are thought to be more than 400 years old.

A review of recent research has shown that the Plumivore will reuse its nest year after year. This species will often renew and rebuild the old nest through substantial repair to save having to replace it. This bird feeds its young on regurgitated feathers, reducing its reliance on legitimate food. The Plumivore is difficult to attract to feeders.

Song variations include the following:

> *"ree ree ree cy cul"*
>
> *"ree ree ree uze"*
>
> *"ree ree ree pair"*

Global Positioning Situator

First North American bird named in the twenty-first century. The Global Positioning Situator always knows where it is located. Recent studies have shown that the Situator uses the age-old idea of triangulation, but has taken this practice to a more sophisticated level, requiring only two of whatever it uses. Scientists have termed this ability "biangulation." As it migrates, the Situator uses the magnetic field of the earth (like other less technically competent migrants), as well as communication satellites and microwave towers. This complex activity provides the bird with constant updates regarding its position with respect to famous landmarks, interstate highways, and rest areas. Situators may be found roaming aimlessly in areas with poor reception.

Like other mimic thrushes, its songs include a variety of sounds, such as bell, chime, old phone, choo choo, digital, robot, sonar, and vibrate.

OBSERVATION HINT

Birders can locate Situators most easily by using Google Earth Nest View.

Hook-billed Crochet

Giant-billed Snapper

This little-known bird with sedentary habits is seldom seen. The Snapper spends most daylight hours with its enormous bill resting in the crotch of a tree. It uses its tongue as a worm-like lure to attract Worm-eating Warblers. The Snapper is highly territorial, with the typical range measuring approximately 9.736 inches by 9.736 inches.

Recently, a subspecies has been discovered near streams in the Rocky Mountains. It is told from the "regular" Snapper by its mayfly-like tongue. This bird feeds primarily on trout.

OBSERVATION HINT

The Giant-billed Snapper relocates its territory at night. It can sometimes be seen in car headlights, dragging its bill along the shoulders of remote roads.

9.736"

9.736"

Range

Tongue detail

Split-winged Swift

This smallish swift is most often identified by its fast and erratic flight, its cigar-shaped body, and its four wings. It is of historical interest that early French Canadian observers nicknamed this bird *Petit Aerodeux* (Little Biplane). The unique wing structure of this species is difficult to observe because of the swift's flight habits, but it can be spotted with a high-speed aeroteledigiphotovideographic camera—or with the bird in hand. This four-wing adaptation likely occurred so that the bird could perform daring stunts during courtship. Recent studies have shown that molting order in the Split-winged Swift is upper left, lower right, lower left, upper right. When not on the wings, this bird spends most of its time preening.

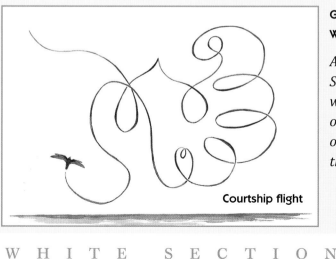

Courtship flight

GOVERNMENT WARNING

According to the Surgeon General, whiplash may occur when observing this bird.

Stunt flying

Spoon-billed Hummingbird

This average-sized hummingbird is easily confused with the more common insectivorous species, the Fork-billed Hummingbird. The Spoon-billed Hummingbird uses its unique beak to squeeze the nectar from flowers. Ornithologists who have observed this behavior say that the Spoon-billed Hummingbird

Spooning flight

is "highly fructosivorous." The aerial courtship display of the male involves rapid flight in an indented oval, commonly called "spooning."

OBSERVATION HINT

Because positive identification cannot be made with a profile view of the bird, best results are obtained if two observers work an area together, moving so as to remain at right angles to each other.

AID IN IDENTIFICATION

Whereas the Fork-billed Hummingbird moves its wings at a rate of 58 beats per second (208,800 beats per hour), the Spoon-billed Hummingbird has a wing beat of 62 beats per second. It helps to count by twos.

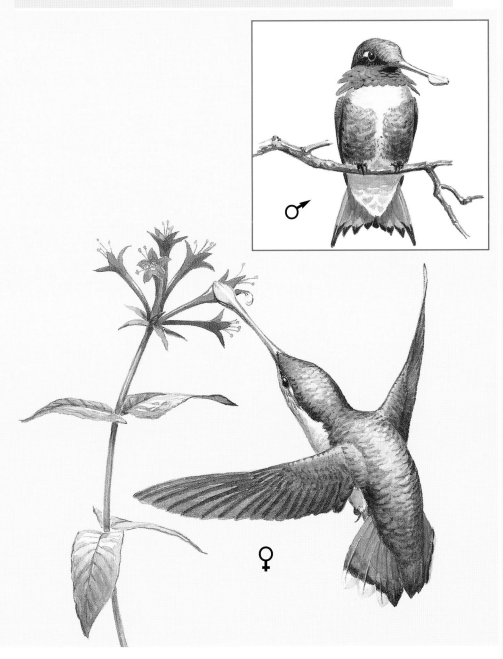

♂

♀

Hook-billed Crochet

This extremely right-brained bird exhibits a behavior new to the annals of contemporary bird lore. Although most birds build nests that are merely functional, these Crochets create beautiful filigreed nests by repeatedly looping strands of spider webs and thin plant fibers into intricate patterns. Different birds use different designs and their nest patterns change from year to year.

It is not clear how they decide on particular designs, but the prevailing theory maintains that this behavior (known as "multivaried nestification") is learned from observation. Crochets are often seen hovering near doily displays in the windows of needlework supply shops.

Call is a sudden, loud *stitchity-stitchity-stitchity*.

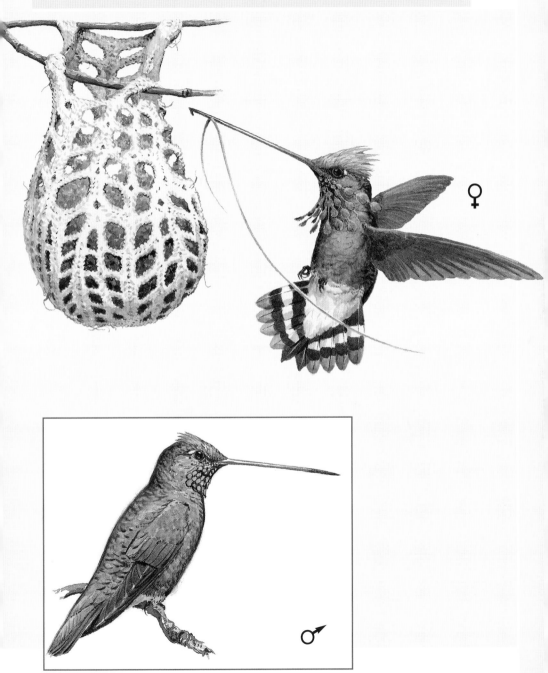

Monarch Warbler

ORANGE SECTION

Small Flycatcher

Named after the little-known and currently dead ornithologist, Dr. Magnus Small, this flycatcher is yet another in the genus *Empidonax*. Because it has no field marks, it is particularly difficult to identify. The best approach is to look at the wings, tail, and feet. However, other parts of the bird can also be looked at if you like. It is so similar to other species in this genus that even individual birds have difficulty with identification, drastically reducing mating opportunities.

Their vocalizations complicate things further. The song of this species is *do-re-mi-fa-sol-la-ti-do*. However, this is the very reason for its low breeding success. The males sing *do-re-mi-fa-sol-la* and the females sing *mi-fa-sol-la-ti-do*. The Vennogram below shows clearly that birds that sing the abbreviated song, *mi-fa-sol-la*, cannot tell each other apart.

OBSERVATION HINT

Most easily identified when birding alone.

AUTHORS' NOTE #1

This bird is just too hard to identify. We recommend that it be deleted from ALL future bird guides.

AUTHORS' NOTE #2

Not all the authors want to delete this bird.

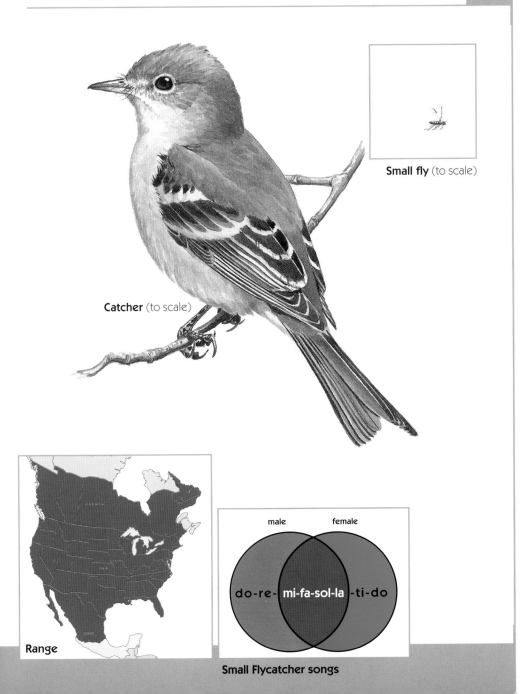

Small fly (to scale)

Catcher (to scale)

male   female

do-re- mi-fa-sol-la -ti-do

Range

Small Flycatcher songs

Gilded Worm Weaver

A species distantly related to both the vireos and warblers, it is most easily identified during the nesting season. This colorful bird constructs its nest of live worms and lines it with wooly caterpillars. Original studies suggested that a great deal of time was devoted to nest repair. As a result, little time was spent on incubating the eggs, so that few breeding successes were reported. More recently it has been learned that nest predation by the nestlings created this problem. Biologists have coined the scientific term "nest consumption" to describe this behavior. Studies show that a typical nest comprises 7 percent Bag Worms, 33 percent Wooly Caterpillars, 22 percent Tent Caterpillars, and 38 percent Wiggle Worms.

Eastern Spider Spitter

Named for its feeding habits, this species spews a spate of speedy, spherical, spinning spitballs spiraling toward spectacularly speckled spiders, slightly smaller (size-wise) than scorpions, stoneflies, and stink bugs. They are often easy to locate since Spider Spitters spew spent spit, splattering spongy spray spots all over the place.

Call is a muffled *spish...spish...spish...spish.*

OBSERVATION HINT

When birding in a group, identifying this bird solely by song is unreliable.

SPECIALIZED EQUIPMENT

Binocular lens cleaning wipes

ADDENDUM

The Association for Precise Nomenclature has recently proposed a new name for the Spitter: the Eastern Arachnid Expectorator. The authors plan to oppose the proposal because the suggested name lacks sufficient alliteration.

Military Warbler

This small, elusive warbler is difficult to find. Apparently evolving as a mutant after early nuclear tests, this bird is now common only on widely

Obsolete plumage

scattered high-security military bases. The tail pattern indicates some sort of social rank. It seems obvious that mutations are continuing; birds recently mist-netted show a change in overall appearance from those captured only a few decades ago. These "new" birds are equally difficult to find.

Song is a bugled *"you can't get 'em up, you can't get 'em up, you can't get 'em up in the morning."* Its call is an abrupt *"ten-hut!"*

OBSERVATION HINT

The Military Warbler is so well camouflaged that it cannot readily be seen. The fact that one cannot see the bird is sufficient proof to list it.

SPECIALIZED WARNING

Being caught on a military base with camera and binoculars is difficult to explain.

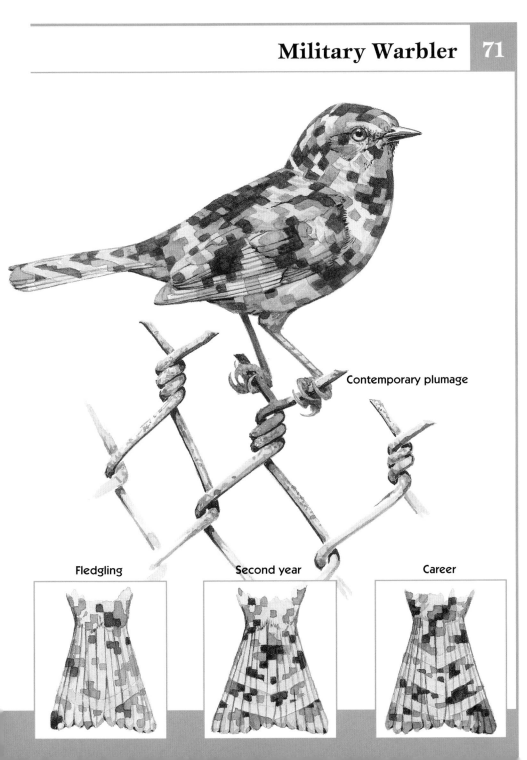

Contemporary plumage

Fledgling

Second year

Career

Monarch Warbler

This brightly colored bird has escaped detection for many years because of its peculiar habit of migrating with large flocks of Monarch Butterflies. While heavier bodied than the Monarchs, the wing pattern of this warbler species is a surprising match to that of the butterfly. Some predators are intimidated since they apparently see this bird as a butterfly on steroids, while others see it as a juicy morsel.

The song of the Monarch Warbler is substantially louder than that of the Monarch Butterfly.

OBSERVATION HINT

This species can best be observed at close range by examining the front grill of your vehicle after driving through a flock of Monarch Butterflies. Remember to drive slowly, since only live specimens can be added to your life list.

AUTHORS' NOTE

Protests by local lepidoptera lover clubs have effectively put a stop to this observation methodology. Individual club members have been known to chain themselves to the grills of birders' vehicles.

Egg

Texas Warbler

The largest member of the genus *Setophaga*, this species is difficult to identify because it is the speediest flier. It is also the most beautiful, has the loudest song, is the most ferocious, and molts the most rapidly. A highly aggressive species, it feeds on tarantulas, bats, and small rattlesnakes.

Song is often likened to the first few bars of "The Yellow Rose of Texas."

OBSERVATION HINT

This species must be viewed flying left to right for the diagnostic ear patch to have the shape shown. If the birds are flying in the other direction, the image must be reversed by viewing them in a fast-focus mirror.

Range

Appetizer course

Greater Wandering Vagrant

Greater Wandering Vagrant

This species is known to wander over much of North America. In the spring, Greater Vagrants arrive in Florida from somewhere and move in an arc before returning somewhere else in the fall. To date, no nesting grounds have been located, and some information indicates that they may carry their nests along on their travels. It is not yet clear how first-year young are imprinted so that they can wander properly.

Song is unusual.

OBSERVATION HINT

Increased border security has substantially affected the southward fall migration. Birds are starting to pile up along the United States–Mexico border.

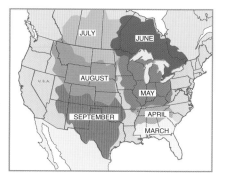

APOLOGY

*When they researched the first edition of this guide, the authors accepted anecdotal evidence that the Vagrant carried its nest along on its wanderings. Later, we mistakenly believed ornithological rumors that the bird carried its young in a pouch and illustrated this behavior in our second guide (*ANOTHER FIELD GUIDE TO LITTLE-KNOWN AND SELDOM-SEEN BIRDS OF NORTH AMERICA*). We were wrong on that occasion and we apologize. Now it is obvious that we were actually right the first time.*

Early theory

Later theory

Current theory

American Bunting

Prairie Molter

The range of this cardinal-sized bird is limited to the few remaining tallgrass prairies in the United States and Canada. Unlike other birds that molt at prescribed times, the Prairie Molter exhibits CFE (continual feather expulsion), exposing the bird's down. As a result, these birds generally look disheveled and their appearances vary depending on which portion of their body is molting. Early settlers were terrified of this bird, fearing that it carried incurable avian mange. In flight, it is identified by the trailing stream of dislodged feathers. Gender dichromism is exhibited through the blue down of the male and the red down of the female. The eggs also molt.

OBSERVATION HINT

Drive 3.26 miles south on Highway 211, turn right and continue for 1.572 miles on County Road SR763 (SR 46 in metric). Immediately past a small unnamed stream, stop at a large pasture on the right. Check the eighth fence post. A Prairie Molter was seen here last year.

Eastern Narrow Sparrow

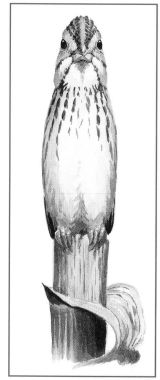

Defense posture

In profile, this bird looks like a typical Savannah Sparrow. However, the body of this species is laterally compressed and abdominally reduced. This species travels in flocks and frequents cut-over cornfields. When alarmed, all individuals turn to face the intruder and freeze in place, thus appearing as a field of stubble.

Song is a single thin whistle.

OBSERVATION HINT

Contact the owners of any field where this species is believed to feed and obtain permission to flush the birds. Because Eastern Narrow Sparrows will maintain their frozen posture for indefinite periods, the most successful means of flushing them is to set the field on fire.

Lesser Shedding Sparrow

This bird was long considered a subspecies of the field sparrow; however, recent studies have shown that it is indeed a separate species. Conclusive identification is quite difficult except during the molting season (first full moon following the second Thursday after the vernal equinox, providing all chance of frost is past). The Shedding Sparrow doesn't actually molt but rather sheds its entire skin, apparently a holdover from its reptilian ancestry. Avian dermatologists refer to this as "instantaneous epidermal exfoliation." If flushed immediately after shedding, this species is easily recognized by its bright pink color.

Spizella nudus often sings exposed on a low perch.

OBSERVATION HINT

Erect a blind in fields identified by the presence of shed skins and wait for the birds to return. They will be walking.

Post shed

Least Minitwit

This smallest of all functioning birds has always been a problem taxonomically because it is so itsy bitsy. The Least Minitwit has evolved protective mimicry and swarms with green bottle flies. Minitwits gather around garbage, walk on ceilings, and buzz in bedrooms after the lights are out.

Their call is an annoying *hmmmmm*.

OBSERVATION HINT

Incredibly close focus binoculars are essential for positive identification.

ADDENDUM

Ornithologists have recently discovered a new population of little flying things that are either a new species of Minitwit, or just a subspecies of the Green Bottle Fly. It was initially designated as the Greater Least Minitwit. However, once the Committee on Confusing Bird Names met, they realized that the words "Greater" and "Mini" and "Least" cancel each other out. As a result, if this is truly a bird, its name will be simply Twit.

Enlarged to show detail

American Bunting

The American Bunting was a common bird in Colonial times. As a result, many of our founding fathers supported this species as our national bird. In the early 1900s, the American Bunting population was decimated by milliners seeking accessories for Independence Day Parade hats. Following the bicentennial festivities of 1976, the population increased, and indications are that it is reclaiming some of its original habitat from the English sparrow. There are now stable colonies in the Philadelphia, Boston, and Washington, D.C., areas.

SONG-O-GRAM

ADDENDUM

Two new subspecies have recently been identified. These have been named the Red States Bunting and Blue States Bunting. Ornithologists have observed conflicts that often result in shrill vocal disputes.

New Bird Record

We have prepared the following sheet to allow birders to record (and thus get credit for) new sightings. To save time, we have already applied for a name and this has been approved by the International Bird Name Company.

COMMON NAME   Chulid Bungolert

LATIN NAME_____*us* _____ *ii*

Note: any words are okay if they end in -*us* or-*ii*.

This bird is about _____ inches tall and _____ cm long.

It has _____ wings, and _____ toes and _____ feathers.

Often found flocking with _____ and cohabitating with _____ ,

this _____ is _____ or _____ and while_____

_____, it often _____ and also _____.

OBSERVATION HINT

This bird can best be observed by

_____,

_____and/or

_____ .

DISCLAIMER

The bird you observe may appear differently than the bird shown

Use only professional grade crayons.

Field Notes (Circle the Correct Answers)

DATE _____   TIME   Eastern Daylight Savings
                                          Central Standard
                                          Rocky Mountain Standard
                                          Pacific Daylight Savings
                                          Arizona Time
                                          Late

SKY CONDITIONS	Clear	Cloudy	Rain	Big
TEMPERATURE	Cold	Hot	Tepid	In car, pleasant

BIRD INFORMATION

HABITAT	Above	Below	Beside	Adjacent
COLOR	Dark	Light	Colorful	Drab
SIZE	Small	Medium	Large	Other
FLYING SPEED	WOW!	Okay	Slow	Stalled
WINGS	1	2	Unsure	Moving too fast to count
LEGS	Right	Left	Both	Neither
SONG	Usual	Unusual	Different	Unfamiliar
FLIGHT DIRECTION	Toward	Away	Sideways	
LOCATION	Hither	Thither	Yon	

OBSERVER COMPETENCY

a) Knows what birds are

b) Recognizes binoculars

c) Knows someone with binoculars

e) Thinks things look farther away through binoculars

f) Thinks things look closer through binoculars

ARE THERE ANY MORE BIRD SPECIES TO DISCOVER?

THIS EMINENTLY REASONABLE question has not been adequately addressed by the ornithological community in the U.S. But after more than five years of thorough and exhausting research, we can now answer this question with a resounding YES!

Drawing on our considerable historical, mathematical, and visual skills, we have compiled the following transpicuous and comprehensible summary of our findings. We relied heavily on the often-overlooked scientific writings of James John Audubon. (Or maybe it was his competitor Alexander Wilson? The handwriting was a bit hard to decipher.) We examined closely the Principle of Habitat Equality, a notion that has for decades been largely ignored. Simply stated, the Principle reads like this: a) Different bird groups use different habitats, AND b) the amount of each habitat available is the same for each group of birds. Consequently, we concluded that it is logical to assume that there should be the same number of species of birds in each group.

However, because the Principle didn't explain how to group birds, we had to figure out how to formulate the groupings. Trained ornithologists like to group birds into categories such as Wading birds, Terns, Owls, Hummingbirds, Jaegers, etc. This creates well over a hundred categories, resulting in much confusion.

By way of a painstakingly tedious examination process, we asked a focus group of people relatively familiar with birds to propose "bird groups." This highly successful effort allowed us to simplify the system and reorganize all North American birds into only twelve groups:

1—*Shore birds*

2—*Ducklike birds*

3—*Birds of prey*

4—*Pelagic birds*

5—*Warblers and vireos*

6—*Sparrowlike birds*

7—*Little birds (titmice, chickadees, hummingbirds, etc.)*

8—*Th- birds (thrushes and thrashers)*

9—*Colorful birds (red/yellow/orange/blue —goldfinches, tanagers, orioles, etc.)*

10—*Black birds (blackbirds, etc.)*

11—*LOUD birds (jays, crows, starlings, etc.)*

12—*Miscellaneous birds (everything else)*

From there it was a simple matter to add up the number of each species in each group and create a bar chart (Figure 1). This colorful graphic clearly demonstrates that the following groups are vastly underrepresented: Little, Th- birds (thrushes and thrashers), Colorful, Black, LOUD, and Miscellaneous.

FIGURE 1

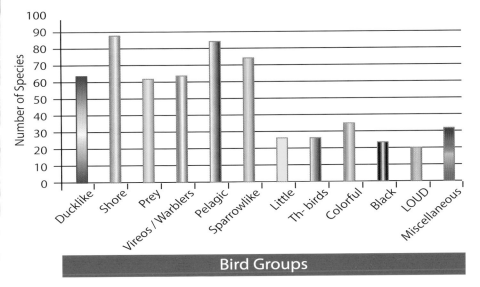

CONCLUSIONS

A—There are more species to be found.

B—The groups where these birds will be discovered are
   Little, Th- Birds, Colorful, Black, LOUD, and Miscellaneous.

C—Audubon was an excellent artist.

GLOSSARY

IN THIS GUIDE, we have made a conscious attempt to avoid ambiguous words or phrases often used in other guides. Below is a short list of ambiguous terms from other guides contrasted with our more lucid terminology.

TERMS FROM OTHER GUIDES	OUR TERMS
Upper breast	Lower neck
Wading bird	Bird with non-webbed feet that walks around in shallow water
Beak	Bill
Bill	Beak
Plumage	Feathers
Soar	Fly around in circles without flapping
Covert	Not used in this guide since we don't know how to pronounce it
Nocturnal migration	Fly by night
Flock	Whole bunch
Chip note	Really, really, really short song
Range	Stove
Subspecies	Species of lesser importance
Evolve	For something that goes around and around what the first time around is called
Pishing	Spishing
Unsure	Conclusive

IDENTIFICATION AIDS

ADVANCED OPTICS:
  Monoculars to Quadrioculars   by Lotta Glass

MYOPIC BIRDER'S GUIDE:
  Near Sightings of Rare Birds   by R. U. Close

TIPS TO SEE MORE BIRDS   by Phillip List

CHASING VAGRANTS   by Willy Findham

PELAGIC BIRDS OF NEBRASKA
  (unabridged and unillustrated)   by Frank Lee Rong

SPECIAL KNOWLEDGE

DEFENDING YOUR SIGHTING   by I. M. Wright and Shirley Knott

PRONUNCIATION GUIDES
  Vol I: Pileated; Vol II: Parula   by Les C. Howe and Jess Wright

BIRD HOUSE FLOOR PLANS   by Archie Tek

TRINOCULARS FOR BETTER BIRDING   by C. Dee Byrde

BIRDS OF THE SOUTHERN SWAMPS   by Anita Bugspreigh

LEISURE

A NEW LOOK AT BIRD MIGRATION   by Ben South

A FLEETING GLIMPSE   by Ima Lister

FOSSIL BIRD SIGHTINGS   by Sutton Stone

EXPOSÉ: CHEATING ON LIFE BIRD LISTS   by Des P. Rett and Iva Gotmore

FINDING 9,236 SPECIES (GIVE OR TAKE)   by Percy V. Rance

BIRDING SECRETS   by Lou Slips

L to R—Ben Sill, John Sill, and
Cathryn Sill, from a bird's-eye view

Alice Dewhurst

BEN SILL

is a retired professor of
engineering at Clemson
University. He lives with his
wife Lois and rescued dogs
Ollie and Jubal in the
foothills of South Carolina
where Ben saw a really neat
yellow bird last year. Like
John and Cathryn, Ben is
an avid birder.

JOHN SILL

has worked as a freelance
artist and illustrator since
1971. While the subjects
for most of John's work
have been birds (both real
and imagined), his illustrations for his wife Cathryn's
much awarded ABOUT
series of children's books
have expanded his work
to include other wildlife.

CATHRYN SILL

is a retired elementary
school teacher who loves
nature. She is the author of
the acclaimed ABOUT series
and the ABOUT HABITATS
series. Cathryn and John
have a home in the woods
where the birding is good.
They live in the mountains
of North Carolina.

PUBLISHER'S NOTE

*Ben, John, and Cathryn have also collaborated on ANOTHER FIELD GUIDE TO
LITTLE-KNOWN AND SELDOM-SEEN BIRDS OF NORTH AMERICA and BEYOND BIRDWATCHING.*